a ballad for
metka krašovec

TOMAŽ ŠALAMUN

a ballad for metka krašovec

translated from the Slovenian by Michael Biggins

TWISTED SPOON PRESS • PRAGUE • 2001

*Publication of this book has been made possible in part by
a grant from the Trubar Foundation, located at
the Association of Slovenian Writers, Ljubljana, Slovenia.*

ISBN 80-86264-12-2

contents

book 2

book 1

This memoir is a hatchet to slash through my own heavy flesh
and through the flesh of anyone else who happens to get in
the way . . . But, you see, this is not fiction. This is life. My
problem is that I don't know what I am doing. I lived all this
mess, but I don't know what it is. I don't even know what I
mean by "it."

Joyce Carol Oates, *Expensive People*

"Nothingness is the source of everything," I say — and
precisely that allows me to stand on it as safely as on concrete.

Emil Filipčič, *Grein vaun*

Night drenches the land of the smile.
Death is in an ant's fist.

I didn't bring dice to the table not to see the cake's bottom.

Escape up the power pillar!
The emperor's servants' door won't yield to dust.

Draw a totem in the nests. The dog will drag off what's there.

Moss is tucked away in dark drawers.

Off with the crackpot's head. His horse eats.

Billions of stalwarts. Too few for a single bird flight.

Who, if he ponders, knows of a tree shooting out of a pumpkin.

Found a green airplane. Throw steaks on the block.

Neither the screen on the window nor the guard at the door cares to hear about one gray kopeck. Each knows the wisdom of both sides.

Father, with your whetted teeth, why don't flowers grow from your flesh?

Questions are the chronic deaths of unmilked animals.
Sight is the punishment.

I don't know what the spirit of silver smells like.

O tribes! Graze your fly on your mouths.
The fortress bursts.
Let the ointment drip on the rounded shapes of the planes.

Yes, said Alice, but that leaves the question of whether time
has a pocket.
Gold needs soap bubbles more than the sky.

Wire the horses. They know what to do with the oats.

The eye washes a wound in the belly. This is where I'm at home.

Shortcuts wash the street. The breath of springtime lingers and stands still.

There are fingers in cups on the altar.
Whoever picks up the pot will boil.

The peaks of the rooftops. See the rope on the branch? Perpendicular from the pine.
Solitude is a shot in the void.

All people don't have a sense of moderation.

Draw fairy tales. I'll be in the picture as punishment.

A photo of the copy will sink any goalie.

Monsters in the gums are crushed into birds' shoes.
Their shin bones stick out.

In the saddle the windows are egg-shaped.

The name is in the whiteness and the jagged w's.

Others rework the factories into rabbits.

There's gold in the seed. Only in snow does it melt into a cult.

The king whispers to the shore.

I don't like black cherries on the tree.
Who rubbed soot on the she bear?
A fetus, smashed jaw bone, part of the wind pipe missing.
I'd like to be rain, scrubbing the roof.
I'd like all my hair to burn, to be bare.
I died when I took my shoes off.
Ivy entwined me, like a castle.
Inside me there's still chalk,
outside a small yellow briefcase.
It dangles from my hand like a saint hanged
from a tree — the same cherry tree.

For David Del Tredici

Whips! Yolks!
The captain threw a lasso and knocked me to the steamship's
bottom.
I'm left alone in these peelings of spring.
My tunic too long. You sting me.
I can't endure with my sleeves rolled up.
God knows where the pianist is.
A door with a brass handle slammed behind him.
The book shelves shook as he started his car.

Sullen is the pose of the black child, bending over the well.
He's eating his scabs.
A glider shoots out of a hangar.
It must be early April.
The child shivers on the stone.
You can see the pilot's leather eyes.
The leather straps under the pilot's chin are
thinner than the rope that drops into the well.

A tiny bug is on the screen of a sifter,
on it a drop of beer.
Next floor up lives a girl with yellow eyes.

It was exactly noon when the sun shone
straight down on my head.
I counted my rings, looked for the shade.
I placed my stamp in the desert.
Then I took a monogrammed handkerchief.
I put it under a waterfall.
It was a minute past noon.
The balance remained the same.

A line-drawing deer swims in the water.
Easter recurs eternally.
A wild boar shakes the trunk of an oak.
Tea spills across the grass.
Numbers are etched in binocular lenses.

On Sundays, when they wrap the bells up in cellophane
and carpenters hammer nails into the wooden wall,
people flow like a stream. Water always
runs downhill.
On Mondays soldiers get dry rations.
They rub cortisone on themselves.
Bunches of hellebores adorn the sleds.

A sword delineates seven things.

Deer, children aren't born from mothers, but from
emptiness. Likewise, lettuce doesn't grow out of the ground,
but from emptiness.

I'm more silent than a snake.

A seed flying off the adhesive tape,
where did I draw a train on the map?
Boughs branches, boughs branches catch the engine's steam.
Turn on the lights.
I see my neighbor's tiny yellow fist.
I imagine the world standing on its tip toes.
Here in the tunnel someone forgot an orange.
Only oil can slip through the sun.
It shines onto a carved bench.

I drink flour out of Meissen saucers.
I never considered that knots are where
branches grow out of the pines.
Why does the flame licking my hand emanate from the eyes
of a man long since dead?
The Danube floods.
All memory is extinguished.

Of all the drenched guests only the oldest
doesn't bother me.
The rest should be shoved in an igloo.
We'll give them marmelade, like last year.
I'm speaking in the future tense.
When we lift all of it up, set it on round
poles and slowly, with horses, move the nests toward the south.

I throb in tiny copper wall tiles.
You've struck me to the quick with that light.
Count the leaves of your life,
you'll see I'm not mistaken.
Only sheep will slip.

epitaph

Only God exists. Spirits are a phantom.
Blind shadows of machines concealing the Kiss.
My Death is my Death. It won't be shared
with the dull peace of others squashed beneath this sod.

Whoever kneels at my grave — take note —
the earth will shake. I'll root up the sweet juices from
your genitals and neck. Give me your mouth.
Take care that no thorns pierce your

eardrums as you writhe, like a worm,
the living before the dead. Let this oxygen
bomb wash you gently. Explode you only

so far as your heart will support. Stand up
and remember. I love everyone who truly knows me.
Always. Get up now. You've pledged yourself and awakened.

A stream,
the scent of freshness.
My tooth starts aching.

All my girlfriends have turned gray.

Dandelion fluff floats.
A stone sinks.
I stare at the circles.

White plates come between the fish and blue tablecloth.

I eat rhubarb and see grandfather's
house with its oleanders and cracked
steps.

Tsilka is forbidden to clean the guns.

Mrs. Abramič is winding wool.

Deer come in the early morning.

German prisoners eat out of tin plates.

The stone, not the mind, draws
circles in the pond.
I wait for the right gesture to straighten my heart.

Birds across the ocean,
the same spoons are here, too.

When I see cakes wrapped up in part
transparent, part frosted paper,
my mouth waters.

I remember a thorn in my heel.
Sheaves of wheat lay in a field.

When I climbed up on my father's shoulders,
I didn't know he would die.

Blue towels terrify me.

The pictures of naked women keep moving
to higher shelves as I grow up.

When father works, the clocks stand still.

The chalk in this picture will have to be fixed.

Even really strange people travel by train.

The world is so big and wide
that we're like little flies.

That taxi driver must have suffered a lot in life,
huh, mommy.

It's composition when the lines blur nicely
and arrive at the same spot on the apple's crust.

They've blocked our radio.

In freedom everyone's eyes will shine.

We'll smooth out foil chocolate wrappers
and roll them up again in tight, tiny balls
for other continents.

Bombs kill grasshoppers, too, if they fall on a meadow.

The children's mouths are smeared with chocolate.
There's a blotter and a bronze horse on the desk.

I look at my white heels.
A mill like the one shepherds make out at pasture.

In the clap of a hand:
countless cow births.

Sorry, pine!
You fall when I write.

Those lines that the lion scented are in the pupil of my eye.

I'd like to die with a red cap on my head.

A fly on the hairs between splayed legs
has no sense of the agony of birth.

In a great wall
a crevice for a white candle.

The number 20.
I've hurt my fist.

The arc of a swaying net retains the same
power of primordial memory as the ash of this box.

Ladders are made of the same rusty points as mud.

A dark, precisely fitted bandage
covers my sun in its golden spot.

I touch the skin:
it doesn't flash.

Deceptions are the deceptions of technology:
of an unformed face.

The wings of a bee torn off:
he pitched wooden hoops onto a bottleneck.

A duck devours mould to keep the species from dying out.

west broadway

I like being in the air. I descend on the city, on
people. Burrow into the ground. Carts with oxen,
a peasant with a whip drives through the village on a peaceful
afternoon. In the Bronx, a Jew dressed like he was
back then. The view onto the roofs of streetcars from
the dentist's in the Ljubljana skyscraper
is gone. They were strange and I was so high
up. Then came the hungry years. I was in places
where people wore black, clinging
trousers. Walls were spattered with red
oxide, the mayor showed us where a giant
power plant would stand. Then we moved to the sea.
Among the bamboo I puzzled where all the pine
needles came from. I watched steam ships
from the terrace. I knew I would sail. They woke me up
in a town where the white sun shone on the Duomo.
The pharmacists whispered. They threw books onto
trucks. They were leaving because we had come.
I don't have a country. Whomever I clutch onto, I drink.
Everywhere they bid bulldozers to tear down my
buildings. This bar and these people walking past —
Castelli, who's aged since I saw him
last — that's when the fire was in Venice, there was
a revolution, although he still has the same
dog, other beautiful women around him, the same kind of
wild orchid in his lapel.

gabrče

A fine thing. The right thing. These dark pine
branches guard what's behind them, color. A bird,
chiseled like a wooden toy — a paper
napkin — if it didn't hop and sing.
A strong desire seizes me to climb up and
set a silver candlestick beside its nest.
A gesture beside the mould of death. These fellows will
grow up into mountains, they'll moulder like abandoned
mills. Will memory ever scatter them over the
earth in the sky? Lojze, Stanko, the innkeeper's
cross-eyed boy. Gone where? I'll be a waiter. I'll be
a woodsman. I'll stay at home on the farm. I'll go
in search of other sunsets, to sea.
Is the line between snow and dry land
sharply defined? Is the Rižana the best place for pitching
banknotes into lard? Will you come back next year?
Are you eating enough meat?

109 = 10 = 1

"I'm on my way, sweet wife, I'm on my way." — The author in a letter to his wife, from Yaddo to Ljubljana, May 15, 1979.

"Cher Maître, nous sommes au mois d'amour; j'ai (presque) dix-sept ans." — Arthur Rimbaud in a letter to Theodore de Banville, May 24, 1870.

"Tomás: quiero vivir mi juventud a tu lado y compartir mi vejéz con la tuya. Siento miedo tan solo de pensar que no regreses y te olvides de mí, y al mismo tiempo espero que los tres meses que faltan para tu regreso pasen rápido." — Alejandro Gallegos Duval in a letter to the author, from Mexico to Ljubljana, March 26, 1979.

Blue circles in the mouth —
garlic for the heart,
wind-blown ashes at the edges of a hexagram —
of years.

When it snows
the earth roars under the weight of oxygen and pain.

A virgin forest,
a water lily floats above the valley.

Little rag girls,
a mother like a clay muzzle.

Blue pencils on a white strip of paper.
The fluttering of a stony horror — cherries.

Fingers on the back of the neck.
The scent of night's infinite infatuation.

Love is in scissors that cut.
Wires that chase sleep away.

Shepherds wait.
Kekec smashes his hand.

Within the mountain —
along a thick, vertical line on the temple's wall —
the burden collapses in cascades of lava.

Butterfly fixed with a silver pin —
the shadow of your wings is now my wellspring.

Swords are for the powerful.
Threads are for pure silk.

I am the mouth of the Book.

Feathers are the feathers of god and dog,
conspiring brothers —
fresh linen.

Bananas,
as real as clouds.

Cockroaches perished in white lime —
a ford of the universe.

A bubble in wet flour bursts —
the illusion of a trolley.

A city of light is built on a cliffside.
The edge of the abyss is too damp.
The first birth has no memory.

Supreme grace opens onto
terror. Every system of death cultivates
material. Poetry is most valued at the
court for performing drudge work.
Kafka is at fault for the occupation of Prague!

Counting is most terrible of all, because it's beyond death.
Roots break the tongue's seed for
tactical reasons of the cosmos.
Work shoots out a crystal kernel — buds of nothingness.
Its status is higher than the status of peacock's feathers.

snow man

Suffering joins fear and disgust.
I see enormous snowballs. I SEE
ENORMOUS SNOWBALLS. People
think they contain the hidden horror
of the world. But I know. They're the finished
work of slaves, waiting for me.
I can build the little guy
half asleep. When I take a red root
from the bin and stick it in the smallest
ball, I'm more relaxed than a
king who's planted a tree. The photos
of my gestures go to the center.
Immortality is always nihilistic.

we peasants

When I truly shifts,
two deer appear to people on earth,
the green forest's color stops dead,
madness swallows us, and drunkenness.

When I truly parts,
I breathe slowly, slowly, gently,
in horror I stare at the tremor, like a pagan,
dumbstruck, so as not to expend the world.

Then I wait, for a long time I wait
for that strange ocean to subside.
All Slovenes building houses have a stroke.

My red roofing tiles, the red tiles of my neighbor
Lojze, building a stall for his livestock,
we both gave you color, color.

the dance

It was humid.
Five p.m. by eyewitness accounts.
My head, black from oxidized carrots,
crashed onto the canvas to bright-sounding
shouts. Ustaša were strolling around
town. Little bread loaf, they beat me up.
Then the Liberation Front actually smuggled me through
Gorjanci in a bread basket.
That's when I saved the first life —
Vojeslav Mole's. In a smart navy
overcoat, I pick daisies and wait for
freedom. I always imagined it as an
explosion at the train station.
A huge orchestra, a ray of
light returning to earth;
my mother barefoot, her hair let
down, winding her way up the stairs to the
bunker. No one escapes my
dance, the dance of the white hare. Fresh
recruits are most startled of all, my brand new
wife for instance, whom I
touched on the Pyramid of the Moon.
She slid from Teotihuacán to
Ljubljana, as if on that tarp
used for saving
Christians. Too late! She made a few more
circles like a drunken fly and then
collapsed into white space with terror
in her neck.
We drank champagne from olden times.
Some elderly woman covered my teeth with rice.

This time I washed my head.
But that doesn't prevent
the cries of my overseas monsters.
I'm at work.
On the way.
I comfort them ALL.

san juán de la cruz and john dilg

My god is a cruel yellow bug,
it settles wherever it wants.
Clown! I don't fall for your tricks
anymore! My god is a thousand flashes in a

single cube of sugar. Now I dip it into
coffee in your castle, just as
fate dealt with your two children, Katrina Trask.
The sugar vanishes, I vanish. I wipe

my forehead. The guests stare and ask
if I'm insane. I come unstuck. And again
it transports me into the fire in the eyes of others.
Into the steely velvet irises of John

Dilg. Every bite in his bread is a
tempest. I bend like a bridge. I'll
endure this joke. Where are you,
grass? I'll wall you up in a bee.

Insects, insects! Striped, smelling
machines! Stay where you
were, friend. Don't stroll over the
abyss of my rights — human fibers.

insects, birds

I feel
the hand of god on my neck.
Who is it that dares to crush my head!
I look at
a dead wasp.
It lies on white paper, under a black
note: Call Junoš.
Print that gesture on me, print it.
God is the Void.
His head: a lump of reeking colt's
flesh. It fell to wolves in the snow.

What do you want
dove, go back to the Hudson!
Don't rip my body with lightning.
The window! Make it stop staring.
I've heard that you have
white hands,
lord of the Void.
I've never seen them.

Endure your crime.

manhattan

I'm crucified.
Between continents.
Between loves.
My nests are in the air.
They burn with a gentle flame.
A white sail hides me from
photographers, Hudson River.
The water is deeper here.
The sky a darker gray.
On the horizon
two blunt pencils.
Dug in.
I won't be coming home.

one, my arm

The Holy Ghost has kissed me.
Far, far off I hear an avalanche.
My fingers pierce a jungle.
A fig tree is growing in this room.

My chest has gone all pink.
My eye is black.
A peacock's tail is growing out of me.
I am the Buddha.

What will become of the horses in the Russian steppe
when charred honey starts to flow?
The bright fluid circulates in the earth's flower,
Blossoms are in green pipes.

Mountains and non-mountains squeezed in one,
my arm, I am in stardust.
My face licked, by whom,
a deer, a cat?

I am
dew in a can which
a child can carry,
I am sweet, white milk.

a ballad for metka krašovec

The last time I ever lost
consciousness was in the evening, the fourth of January, in
Mexico. Dr. Sava was treating me
to dinner,
to Benito Cereno,
to the desert,
to Nolde's youth and
to the story of how he'd joined
the Melville Society right before
Borges, when he was buying
grease for Yugoslavia.
Once we published together in Gradina.
Hello, Niš!
But I really couldn't
listen, because I was constantly thinking about
the letter I'd gotten that morning from Metka
Krašovec. A tiny blue letter
written in the same characters as these.
I collapsed under the table.
The next morning I visited her in the
hotel. First, I wadded up some super down
Krašovec for her, some
fiancé three times removed.
He flew right back to LA. I don't
like incest. I put on my
backpack. I kept trying to figure out why I'd
passed out. For weeks I took her around on
buses and gave her everything
to eat: holy
mushrooms and the Pyramid of the Moon. With me you sleep
on hard floors among

scorpions, but also where you pick
fruit and murmur: you are color, you are color.
One day I
interrupted: I've got to go
to Guatemala with that boy, don't you see that he
appeared to me as Christ. We lay on a beach in
the Caribbean, the two of us and a Portuguese whose name
I forgot. Go, she said. I can tell I'll be
crushed, but then I'll merge with you
in the light again. I was
afraid. I went nowhere. And that night I took her to a
motel that was a collection
point for white cargo on the way to Rio.
She kept gazing calmly into my eyes.
You'd better look at the sky, woman, what are you looking
for here, I shouted, I told you long
ago, there's nothing left
here. I was shaking when we reached
the Pacific. Salina Cruz, the fans,
prisoners weaving
a net. I roamed naked through the sand.
Purple plastic bags, the sky, my body, all
purple. Metka! I said to her, you
can't pretend you don't know.
You do! Don't play with fire!
Go back to your
Academy. Eventually they'll even blame me for
making you leave. I have to work,
you take this trip alone, I told
her as we flew back from
Cancún. Why do you lose your
scent and taste, religion!
You're crazy! I shouted at Carlos, Enrique and
Roberto, do you want that woman to

abduct me back
to Slavdom? And why are you looking
so good, she asked me when she came back from
Morelia. And I no longer
knew who was grandma and who was
the wolf. You'll miss your meetings, it's time for you to leave,
Metka! And I saw her to the
airport. I was afraid she'd
explode it with her convulsive
crying. So long! But then the ground
started giving way beneath my feet, too.
My advice that she
pretend I was nearby in Šiška was really
false. Nobody has been in Šiška for ages.
I phoned her.
I'm coming to get married.
Come then, she said calmly.
Through the receiver I could feel her gazing in my eyes.
A very, very
tall gentleman read
my tarot cards, an old woman from
Persia read my palm.
They all told me the same thing.
And I was happy. I shivered.
And I knocked on the
door of my neighbor,
Alejandro Gallegos Duval, to tell him that I was
happy and shivering.

Why are we all living on top of each other?
Junoš and Maja said:
he's not so terribly handsome as you see him, but
it's strange. He looks a lot like Metka
Krašovec. I arrived in Ljubljana on March

twenty-seventh. I paid thirty-two marks for the
cab. Metka was sick and pale.
I returned the blood to her face. And she wouldn't let me
wear his ring, too, but she wanted me to wear
hers alone.
I watched my wedding witnesses with
interest. I finished all the other guests'
sparkling drinks. Did you at least
buy some nice tent with the money from my
Montenegrin reading? Two deer came out
on Snežnik.
I'm here.
My hands shine.
America is my fate.

                              — In the woods of Saratoga, May 1979

A book of photographs:
a tale of the perfect lover.

Learn from the eye of others.

God is my
reader.

to david

Son! I don't see you,
don't hear you.
I caught sight of a squirrel in the
woods as I carried my black
box. Now I'm staring at an
arrow and the label
MARGIN.
Don't collapse into beauty.
Dive into it like an olympic
pool and pierce it from
below.
The surface is beauty.
Let it bleed.

mitla

I forget what I drank in
Mitla.
I remember we wandered onto
side paths,
up the steps.
The stones in the temple were arranged
like a wall with a secret panel
for the hidden image
of a dog's lacerated muzzle.
The dog licked pink sugar
in its mouth.

To the nun who fixed
real hair onto the doll of Christ —
what did you pierce the head with?

Young ladies in far-off lands wear high heels.
Man strokes
a copper sphere.

I set a
dead
anopheles onto velvet, to think more easily about the world's
impermanence.
From a greasy, black field I hear the cry
of a horn.
A cupola smokes.

If it weren't for Descartes, they'd have
found the golden flower!
Horses in the steppes would have their hooves wrapped
in a layer of nylon. The nylon would be in my
mothers' flesh.

I lifted the eastern edge
of the table, to let the
crumbs
of bread roll toward the
door.

When I crawl around
this forest, naked, like
an animal,

I Feel the World.

I will change into
the grasses.
When I am eaten up by

the worms,
they will turn everything,
as I do,

into gold.

With my tongue,
like a faithful, devoted
dog, I lick Your
golden head,
reader.
Horrible is my
love.

god's straw

"La sainte eut d'abord la vie d'une femme entourée
d'un luxe frivole. Elle vécut maritalement, eut
plusieurs fils et n'ignora pas la brûlure de la chair.
En 1285, agée de trente-sept ans, elle changea de vie . . ."
— Georges Bataille, *L'expérience intérieure*

May 22, 9:30, listen
Metka,
wretched creature, lurking from your ambush across
the ocean on my holy mouth with warm, dangling
members, affixed to that infamous
hen-house, dripping with oil and melon.
Into your blind alley, march!
Long live Agatha Christie and all tranquil
fossils! Disgusting
zipper!
Absurdly soldered flour-box, consuming
miles of my paper, even in my
sleep! Where did you get the right
to wiggle beneath me,
paramecium,
to quiver and yelp like the orgasm of some alpine
tour?
Your ears are flat! At every
throb I pray for an avalanche to
bury you. Hey, Saint
Bernards! I want your liquor for my wife. For
her sake I've neglected the
insects that have stopped
fluttering around my silk. Watch yourself,
cannibal, wanting to imprint

my face into your live
flesh.
I won't take the bait.
I'm not some Slovene peasant.
I'm Angelica da Foligno.
I remain god's straw.

andraž and tomaž šalamun

Andraž and Tomaž Šalamun,
sitting in green armchairs,
two awesome salesmen from the least.
(I meant to write from the east,
but mistyped.)
He with his madness,
I with my Christ.
Both of us stare at the smoke.

Yeah, I fuck his brain.
He loves my cries.
(I meant to write Christ,
but mistyped,
word of honor in both
cases.)
The same, mum!

ragtime

Gods,
my thanks to you.

You've given me
a book.

My flight to
Mexico City is AM 405

I'll just take a shower,
to pick up the money,

to fuck
Alejandro Gallegos Duval.

book 2

big deal

It rains, it rains,
my soul is Raskolnikov's soul.
I've cast my people through the air
like a huge bird squirting color.

I'm a criminal, just as outside Hess's
door my guards change.
But Hess has his home in Spandau.
I'm confined to my castle of choice.

The Piranesis no longer comfort me, nor
the Smyrna carpets. Even less, that you also
farted around here like some Ford Maddox Ford,
Louis Adamič. Stella was

mad about your black brother in
Dolenjsko. At first it was like a
fairy tale. But going back, in mid-Atlantic you
wrote: my people are in the scorpion's maw.

Your folks, son of Adam, smoked
you in a shed in mid-America. By
way of ensuring: 1) that you wouldn't get homesick,
2) that you'd remember your Mudville.

telegram

Sí, hasta julio,
Junoš, I hear
sawing in the

forest. It rains sound here. Yeast
rises.   What collapses into
toads and parachutes? In short, damp

wafers form
a roof for
a figure in

a cloak which is
a yellow
dot.   Where?

Not, most likely, on
the canvas. We only see
the sky.

If little men
make order in
our stomachs,

there must be some
lift that raises them to
eye level.

rites over charred remains

Out of the butter of
Blato, your Mudville. Nomina sunt consequentia
rerum.

I look at a log
in the fire. I stuff Adamič into a little
cup. I kick him over the
fire, into the smoke.
He's still burning.

He shaves and exercises.
His tissue pulls away in sizzling
bubbles. Then I take a
glass of port
and douse the
fat man's panic.
The wood hisses. There. I've put you out now,
moron.

bathtub army

Often when I've traveled with my huge
yellow bicycle around the shell of
America and slept in motels where next to
the lamp on a pale violet night
stand there was usually a Bible on a chain I've
thought that these days besides me
there probably aren't many people in the world
who within their children's lifetime stand a
real chance of having their country nail their
poetry on a chain to bedsides which will certainly
happen in Slovenia with my poems
because by then even we will have quite a few
motels.

juice of oranges

I'm exhausted. The grass is gray with
dew after a long night. The pines are
ballerinas. I forgot my lunchbox
in the room. If the wind were to

stop, the cloud would fall in the pond.
My boot is dark brown from the
water in the ground, which comes from the sky.
I'm distracted and infected by the halo.

Surely I'd be more faithful than
a Tang dynasty monk. Loves
which go streaming past so quickly. Death is

a strange drink. Like pinned scraps of paper at
a tailor's, outlined with chalk.
Like white clouds ringing the tops of pines.

sayings of the world

Once long, long
ago I stopped by
Milčinski Street.

A young fellow was
drying a stocking
on the tile stove.

Then I said to
Maruška, hey, let's bet
I know who your

next love will be.
I was so convinced
that I proposed

to write down your
name, seal the envelope, take it to
the bank, and I also

wanted David to
end up with that
chain. For us

to see years
later. Where are you today,
Bojan

Baskar, now that I've
remembered you in Yaddo. Nil,
too, how are you!

memory

In the cry
of heaven I hear
the deadly

silence
of birth
impressing itself

on people and
animals. I
rave in

the snow. My
tracks water
the mind

of the masters.
An insect slices through
the air and

leaves.

I'm suffused with
pleasure in an instant, when I think
how I've broken
all my wives'
hearts.

by jove, here we go again

Speak! Who are you?
Do you kill because you want to be killed and
loved?
Sure, that probably plays a part.
Each human leaks, the flesh is weak.
I am a canvas. I catch light,
returning it to where it came from.
If I hadn't met you, I would have met somebody
else. Do you think the
light that your face is reflecting
will be memorized?
Everything withers away if it isn't fed.
We're in Mexico, aren't we?
"The sun would collapse." Even the
guidebook spells it out clearly.
Do you suppose, then, that you even have
a right to your eyes, like some underaged
beetle? Jove comes from Jupiter,
Jovis. There's nothing innocent
about me. Even if I take
a newspaper and rewrite it, what comes out
is what is. Look, where it says:
Careful! This will make you gasp!

problems and mysticism

Taras relates that
Slodnjak writes that
Cankar's women
told him that he
kicked them. And that this made him a great
mystic. I couldn't say, since I haven't
read him. My grandmother, the late
Jelka Šalamun, née Toplak, simply
slapped him. He was drunk and
shameless when he and Kraigher
came to visit. For me, the only
mystical thing about Cankar was
the fact that during the war
when grandfather was
interned in Serbia, some Nazi
bigshot who was
living in his villa in
Ptuj bought the complete Schwentner
edition at a price that was high
even for then. What a
difference between grandpa, who got turned on by Cankar about
as much as I do, and Herr
Brunner, who clearly prized
the culture of a small
nation. I sold the set to Trubar's
Antiquarian. I can't recall
what I used the money for.
Just as mystical are the passions of
empires. For instance last
month, when the Slavists' conference in
Minnesota hashed through Chekhov, Solovyov,

Solzhenitsyn, Mayakovsky, Cankar and
me. I resent being chased all
the way here by that bewildered
Slovenian soul. So I hold firmly to the
tradition of my clan. On the
dust jacket I've put my grandfather,
armed. While those two pale and pampered
hippies in the foreground are my father
and uncle.

the oeuvre and its brackets

Let various Marxists and the herd still
shuffling outside my door gnash their
teeth, but I'm living
now. All I
do is slightly
rearrange the struggle for the seed flowing
in the universe.
Remember how Maruška
went around dressed!
A fatter rope around
her waist — three years later it appeared in
Vogue — than
the kind they use to dock
a steamship. One day Metka will
show up at the Academy in
sackcloth, tongues of flame shooting from
her eyes. My wives
vie with the Lord
for disguises.
Right at the edge they scream.
They excise me from the head of the world. That's why
this time the muses dictate practical
instructions to me, because they want me to be
fine, even when I'm old and
dottering. With everything cooked
and laundered just right, young poets and lovers
met nicely at the door.
And not a day's delay with correspondence.
In short, my wives must leap into
the Void, but
not with their eyes

closed, or holding their noses from violent
love.
Clearly, that technique only leads to an awful
kerplunk!

Not just me.
Everyone I touch becomes
the food of this flame.

letters to my wife

I

I will be shot
on a day
that is
compact and
fresh.

II

Say hello to Darko if he comes around.
I am your son.
I am your
black star.

III

I look at a female that
glares
insanely,
smoking furiously.

IV

The ladybug earns
a patchwork for every
black
and red dot.

V

The tribe of the
Book gnaws bones into gelatine
and marmelade.
Nature goes in the
other direction.

VI

I think
tortoises
live so long
because they don't see
color.

VII

To die touching skin.
To see mountains out the window.
To cut into flesh and blood of what the wind carries off.
This is my time.

VIII

Beautiful forms contain a hidden
wound.
Streams and fields are on
boards.
Back then there were no
bridges of reinforced concrete. If
the heart doesn't look out
through the arches, it looks
nowhere.
Stigmata are a domestication and
forgetting.

so what did i do in new york?

First: six days with no
mail!?
All kinds of things. Bought books. Put
Alejandro's ring on
my right middle finger.
I want to wear them both. Phoned Curt and
Hortense. Spoke to a
woman with a curly-haired
child and listened to her
life story late into the night.
Watched Woody Allen's Manhattan twice,
and twice got up and clapped.
Danced wildly way at the end of
Christopher Street near the docks and sniffed
poppers. Called a
cab and went to Club 24, First
Avenue. No more discount for me, even if I
lie,
anyone can see how much I've aged.
Asked a doctor if maybe I haven't caught
syphilis, now that I've married
you. Slept with Larry, an incredibly nice
23-year-old black man studying
law.
He didn't smell a bit.
We laughed our heads off. And then slid into
the pool like a couple of relaxed, naked
cows and serenely watched the
other people. Thought: you'd really
lose it, if you knew.
Less than a month after the wedding!

By the way, David Ray, do you think I will be
shot for this in Yugoslavia? Was a little
amazed at myself, a little
appalled, quite happy. The first three weeks I
didn't miss you,
now I miss you, as I
write this. Yes, Metka, I really
mean this, I live and work faithfully and
devoutly. What else? Endlessly debated whether I should
buy running shoes, and still
haven't decided, one of Vivien's shoes
pinches. Yesterday Junoš
wrote me. They've moved Ferdo to
Salina Cruz, into the room where I used
to be, because Maja's mother
has come, so "they can keep better tabs
on me." He must have gone
crazy. Sometimes I feel such
infinite sadness. You Slovenes are so obsessed
with property. What will become of your
paintings if you
constantly whine at me, spinach yes, carrots
no. Was it you who wrote him to make
sure I don't get together with
Alejandro? Sometimes I suspect you of all kinds
of idiocy.
Write to me, Christ, God!

i'll write you a sonnet

Little bourgeois girl, what were you thinking of,
marrying a poet? What is this business about betrayal,
and that your head aches? Fuentes decided that after his
fiftieth birthday he would no longer: change wives, grant

interviews, make awards. Just two minutes
ago I paced through the room furiously wondering
if I should decide the same. My father decided to
learn to type before his fortieth birthday.

Can you imagine! To write all of your correspondence
at home! Well, my Malinche, in case you've decided
to play that kind of trick on your endangered Aztecs,

remember why I've come among you. To teach
you to use a chamber pot, watch the movies, and perfect
the race. It's obvious the gold goes back to Spain!

In hell they eat nuts that they've smashed on a rock.
Even there they keep a diary.

A cow moos.
The mountain that hears it, smashes it.

The mountain crumbles to bits.
A bird now hovers over it to drink water.

The process censors the material.

The people who in one way
or another have passed through me
fuel the earth,
they fuel its beads of sweat.

Love is pain.
The complete absence of what hurts.

Golden rays, I've trimmed you.
The darkness takes care of itself.

Don't fool yourselves.
Even when I sit silent and smoke
stars are extinguished.
I've given no one anything for free.

Of all forms of glass
laughter is the closest to death.

Whoever has seen a bow for him smile
will not forget what was there
before I touched the clay.

Anyhow, look at the back cover!

doubting grandson

"Children, go to sleep on the train from Trieste to Vienna. There's nothing to see along the way."
— my grandmother Mila Gulič, 1891-1978

Don't nod off on
the train from Venice to
Vienna, dear
reader.
Slovenia is so
tiny you could
miss it. Tinier than my
ranch east of the
Sierras!
Instead, get up,
stick your head out the window, though it says
FORBIDDEN!
Listen to my
golden voice!

prologue I

God is made of wood and doused in gasoline.
I take a cigarette to burn a spider's leg.

The gentle swaying of grasses in the wind.
Heaven's vault is cruel.

prologue II

I write this to you, whom till now I've only
warned.
I can scarcely control my
servants, who threaten me with
revolt.

The smell of your burnt
flesh is my
life, they whisper.
We're too old to
change masters.

So I warn you, your fate is
not clear.
If I weary in
this battle, you'll
burn up.

a prayer

Friend!
Have you ever experienced
the endless pleasure of stars
merging,
the pop of a flower when it
unfolds in a red
horizon?
Don't underrate the most
horrific esthetic
pleasures.
Every day, every
minute I fight
for you.
Thank you for your
name.
My ultimate
ally in the struggle for your
life.
Plead for me.
Plead that my foe not dim
my wits and drag
me off, innocent, to the
machine.
Plead that I master time
in my sleep and keep you alive
with silence.

god

I
demand
unconditional
love
and
complete
freedom.
That is why
I am
terrible.

sixth of june

Cover your
eyes, friend!
Don't look at me!
Shield your
gaze —
a bridge of death.
In the woods I hear
a saw.
My light is
yellow.
My ribbon is
black and
red.
I watch over you.

poetry

It is
a greater
pleasure
to lose
women
than
money.
The greatest
pleasure
is
to lose
your own
death.

metka

I'm as
sleepy
as a
child.
I love
you
and the
whole
world
alike.

the man from galilee

My chair.
It's true!
A fly has as much right to write the history of biology.

I smoke and
look at the photo above the calendar.
Women don't tire.

Silently I gnaw at
an apple and throw it in the trash.
A stone dropped in a pond.

Monstrous Victorian
heads on the lampshade.
Who invented glass!

I rub my eyes
and play with my pee-pee.
Today I'll go to bed happy.

I wonder what kind of
minority I'd have to be, if my legs were so
huge they stuck out 14 inches past
my brass bedpost.

de rerum naturae

Dear grandma, even now I remember your gentle
advice: be kind and
polite to the lower
classes. They're people too. Common
folk can offer a wealth of
lessons. Yes, Lenin. That's why
I swear in my poems.
In the Second World War, rampaging
Slavs ripped up my coat on Ilica and trampled
my fur.
Sooner or later everything works out.
A smile and silence are power.
They'll give us back everything they took.
The last carpets went with my good
upbringing when I published my
Poker, just in the first round. And
Papa's last forests, so he could pay off a debt to
Uncle Tozzi, before he wooded the Karst.
Clearly, as a Slovene poet I come across socially
deafer than Beethoven. The only difference is that
his ears got him screwed over by the
Party.

My grandma
could never remember
the names of my schoolmates.
They were:
1. the curly one,
2. the squirmy one,
3. the one whose mother wears too much makeup,
4. the one who always says hello so nicely.

riko adamič!

Remember how we built
a nine-room house with Fructus
crates! How your father's
workers thought we were
childish? And we never published
the novel Wacha-too, which we typed in the
shade, under the laurel tree in our
garden. And how grandma always
asked, so does that mean Riko isn't
the curly one? And we all answered
in chorus: yes, grandma, Riko
is curly, but he's not the one you
think. Riko's the one who
always says hello nicely. And
grandma said,
that's right, two of you are curly-headed. I never know
which is which.
Then the child on duty cleared
the dishes from the table and each of us
went to his corner to
"take a nice nap."

marko

And just as I was
wondering whether our snake
was still alive — we had all been
worried, because it had been
a week since it had touched
any milk — the door bell rang.
On the stairway stood
a woman clutching at her
heart. "Marko doesn't have a father anymore."
I didn't understand. I thought about how
right I was to oppose
ash blue for the
door. You have to
insist, or there will be
scenes. At the top of the stairway Mother
appeared. I went
without a word straight to the basement
and the snake. I sat down on some
logs.
This snake will die, too, because I read too much
Proust. I decided to give up playing
the piano. To be
a better Boy Scout.
I've always wanted Yugoslavia
to win.

astonished eyes

Katka, the A student, got
ASTONISHED EYES. Tomaž, the A student,
got ASTONISHED EYES. Katka,
the pingpong champion, got
ASTONISHED EYES. Tomaž, the sailing enthusiast,
got ASTONISHED EYES. Katka,
Grandfather Frost of the fourteenth precinct,
got ASTONISHED EYES. Andraž,
the A student, got ASTONISHED EYES.
I've gone half a year now with no new
ASTONISHED EYES. Andraž, the violinist,
got ASTONISHED EYES. Father
keeps forgetting what he's bought,
so there are four copies from
him personally.
Dear France Bevk, fellow native of the coast region!
There are twelve copies of your book
in our house and
we still can't get enough!

light not fed by light

Scent of flowering buckwheat,
why do you lure Transylvanian vampires?
Scissors are a painful tool.
No one has the right to crush a stone,

move a doorway from east to north.
But still the archaeologists find forged
iron. How to crush responsibility?
Unchecked, it grows into pandemonium. The creature that

first stared into a fire was fried —
the flame was terrible even in the rain —
and it wanted the fire for itself. Fate is in desire.

The trees burned blissfully. Whoever saves
his life will be spared. Only the one who
splits the mirror with a diamond can sleep soundly.

the boat

Genesis is tiny silken
shifts, thinner than
the nail of your little finger. Are earthquakes and wars
the collapse of galaxies? A couple of swipes
with a brush at the earth's skin,
a diary?
What is minimal?
What proves
the madness of a bud opening,
of a deer grazing? The poet bestows
wreathes, lays on hands. Yet only he who
veils his vision survives.
He who has seen too much has his eyes
pecked out by crows, and
rightfully so. The poet
kills the deer.

jerusalem

The crime has been written:
you will never
meet a person that you
love as much as
me.

kami

— *For Allan Gurganus*

Mandelshtam lives on this continent now.
O, photographs of Russian heads, of onions against
clouds, of cattle in dust. I listen.
I listen for the night to deepen. Allan

tells a story of his mother. For her
coming-out party his grandfather commissioned
a fleet of pink airplanes and pitched pink,
sound-proof tents on the white sand strewn

for the occasion along the Gulf Coast and
summoned Miles Davis. The guests
lost a couple hundred thousand dollars
in jewelry as they danced. What is the door

like of the place where the old woman lived in Odessa?
Made of logs? And where does your name come from?
I've never asked you. Next week
the horse races start. Here and in

Mexico. Sephardim will be drinking milk at
tables along Broadway in this town.
This year it's the fashion to go shirtless,
to have a German shepherd on a leash, in Saratoga.

the tree

— *For P. T. F.*

I'll see you again in March next year. But
the woods will be different. The light will be
different. The leaves will glint,
washed by humidity and sun. The taste of

meat is more terrible in California
than here, in the woods of Saratoga. We wave
to each other now, as I walk toward the castle. With one
hand you chase mosquitos away, with the other you

endlessly paint the same tree. Your loves are
the same as Metka's. Vermeer, Petrus Christus,
the Dahlem Museum. "And when I walked along the beaches
in Delaware, I also remembered

Holland." You say you live in a cabin. The tree
inhabits, becomes you. You wear the same jewelry as my
wife. What stands out on white paper,
nature? And why do you whisper so

softly when you show us your slides? We're only
passers-by here, the Piranesi graphics and your
pictures. Don't be afraid and don't resent me. I
also speak the language of your forebears, Polish.

a stroll in the zoo

I

In Ljubljana
in the zoo there's a
seal.

When it breathes,
it hides. My two
children

put their
hands in animals'
mouths.

Then I say,
David, tell me
something, did

Srečko
really get his hair cut?
Were you

afraid at all
in the airplane
way up high?

II

I run to
buy young
corn.

We'll feed it
to the camel. Just see
what all

a camel
will eat. What an
unusual creature,

always hungry.
Then I remember
Vito.

Sorry!
Back then, when I
helped you move, I was

wounded and
jealous. That
shot in your

gut outside the
Academy, after we'd
driven

around
some barriers in
the dark —

I'd like
to take it out and
sew it shut.

III

Alejandro
has drawn himself
so I can

feel him
more deeply. In the letter
Te quiero

is surrounded
with the same electric
cloud

as in
olden days
the ad for

Ilirija
shoe wax. Good god,
now I have a wife

again. I doubt
she'll allow me
these things

at all.
Then Ana
laughs.

Tomaž, Pepca
said we have to
be back by twelve

thirty. And you
go off daydreaming
in the zoo.

IV

Metka, I said,
at the zoo
I saw

a llama.
Did you ever read
about millionaires

in South
America who go
to bed with those

animals? Before
I didn't understand.
This

afternoon,
when I looked in
its eyes,

I was
shaken, too. Just
what we

needed,
Metka says. With
a llama! Aren't

things
bad enough?
And I

remember
Maruška, who was
afraid

I'd go to
bed with Ana.
Women are

afraid of
a million
things.

circles

My
rings are
yellow

gold,
white gold and
silver.

I have wives under
glaciers and amid
palm trees.

Who pays
me for this kind
of life?

My
Slovenian nation? My
Slovenian

nation
knows what it's doing. And any
enemy

who plans
to mess with my Slovenian
nation has been

forewarned.
It's a fact: whatever I
write

really *happens*.
His head will fall off
at once.

three poems for miriam

I

I look at
Miriam in the morning, as she
awakens in

Japan. I don't know
the face sleeping beside you in
the bed.

Do you still
wake up first? I picked up
the bright, left

wall, and
from the left only heard noise from the
street. Who is this

fellow? Do you
remember when we ate
frogs

and I was
hungry all
summer?

II

And I
stopped by your atelier on
Veselova Street downstairs from

Kardelj's cook — you said she was
"nice, not at all what you'd
expected" —

and we
danced to the Doors.
Are you still that

quick? When I
saw you safely ensconced
under nicely tanned

muscles —
hardened from digging
with archeologists — I

focused on
Iztok. We'd gotten fairly
warmed up and

undressed. And you
forgot about your prey
and explored me.

I giggled in
bliss, but couldn't get it
up. You

have to
whine in my ear: I want to be your
wife. My

upbringing is
at fault, so I have a cupboard full
of wives and other

corpses
and keep collecting
them.

III

Hey!
When you get back from
Japan

I'd like to ask you
something. How do you explain that
just as I was

pondering
night and day whether I should or I shouldn't —
remember the Bakery? — up

against my thighs there
leaned this dark one, with tight
curly hair, like some Styrian

baroque
Christ. Jesus, how I felt
it. Was that your boyfriend

Gregor? If you're there
together now, say hello to
Kyoto.

I am
KAMI, come to visit you
again.

bob!

At breakfast
Kay Burford,
Kathy's mom,
gave me
"A Cloud in Trousers,"
which you and
Kathy translated in
Iowa in 1972.

Mayakovsky died at 37.

I'm still alive and
sing the world
in gratitude. I've met
some brighter circles
for living.
One of those is
you. And you,
Vladimir.

If we'd made
love in 1930,
you wouldn't have
shot yourself. Why
didn't we?

I stood between
Gayatri and Lili
Brik.

thirty-seven and you twenty-one

Still between life
and death.
My loves are
terrible.
The moon is full.
I'm afraid I'll spill my
port on the terrace.
I'm looking at you, Pavček.
I want money
for my books from you.
My butler
seduces me.
A curse on the day when I decided
to hire too young a butler in Mexico!
Where are you now, my wives?
Wounded? Heartless?
I run out of
fingers counting who all I've crushed.
Like bread.
I'm naked.
But my time still hasn't
come.

why do you tremble, alejandro gallegos duval!

You've all been
nice to me.
My life has been
straighter than my penis
just now. I don't know who has determined it and
set it down. I thank you, though.
When I'm in Mexico, I'll love you to death.
But you stay there for now.
Don't drink your wine too fast, boy.
You've got to become a great painter.
Shut out the noise from the street.
Don't complain I've made you
lose weight, don't show the dark
circles under your eyes.
I've enriched
everyone who has seen me.
Even a blind man would see the dew on the grass,
the milk along my iron path.

to pavček

Perhaps I'll come.
Then again, perhaps I won't.
In any case prepare the
money, since here's my will.
Everything goes to my children.
I've paid Maruška to the
end of October 1979,
and if it's
less than 400 dollars a
month, the Russians will
occupy you.
Study my life
closely. This amount is the
limit of your curse.
Now, at this instant, I still
see him. He's still breathing, still
twitching.
We're in a fleabag hotel
called the Daniel.
The other rooms are filled with
American tourists chewing their dreams.
The company I flew here with is called
Liberty, and
the agent who sent me the
tickets from Albany to Yaddo, Betsy.
I remembered that I hadn't bought
Metka that part for the
cooker she used to
fix me meat, until something
burst and that
safety plug hit the
ceiling.

gaza

When I'm 37 years old, I won't be
bald. I won't
wear white dressing gowns with red
innards bulging in the pockets.
When I'm 37 years old, my
mother won't die. I
won't knock on my sons' bedroom doors with
idiotic questions on my idiotically happy
face.
When I'm 37 years old, I
won't exercise at five-thirty
each morning and wheeze through my nose like a
maniac. I
won't parade through country
inns and insult good
folk who barely survived the
war. I
won't wear knickers. I
won't point to Haloze and all they took
from us and say
it's fine.
When I'm 37 years old, I
won't be on call, I'll be
free. I'll grow a long beard and long
nails, my
white ships will sail all the world's
seas.

And if some
woman bears me children, I'll fling them through the
windowpane from the dining room's
left corner and I
wonder what will hit the asphalt first,
the curtain or the glass.

my uncle jockey and the butcher in zone a

And when we all
returned, happy and windblown, from Montebello —
we'd briefly forgotten the low
prices caused by the disgusting competition of the Yugoslav
border — we said, Uncle Mario didn't just
race, he also
won!
Then I stared at the tunnel
from the window at Piazza Vico 6.
Why don't we have horse
races?
Why did Uncle Jakob sell his
cafe?
Why did grandpa smoke so much that he got
cancer?
And who will inherit
the last wooded parcels?
But soon it got
dark
and next morning the car wouldn't
start.
I had to go crawling uphill in a
bus full of squealing old
women with lire stuffed under their
bras from the chickens they'd
sold. To gape dimwittedly into
my plastic bag. We're going back to the
country where my father's director of coast
region hospitals. He squeals with
delight whenever some woman gives
birth. He must think that way we'll get more
neon.

the koper-saratoga springs axis

Because my father was such a
snob that he refused to be
paid, one day, when
I came home for ten
minutes to shower after a
match, it suddenly became clear
that I would
"just go to Ljubljana" for college.
Serves your inflated ego
right, the family said out loud.
Just who do you think you are! You even
lost to Karlovac. Up to a
point! That's right, we lost to
Karlovac. Which is why I'm here. To
wash up. Back then we all still used
those sprays, I put a fresh
shirt on and joined them at the
table. Wow! I said. Has Mussolini been burning
your banks again? You want to send
me someplace where it's perfectly
clear all I can do is die, rot, become impoverished and
turn gray? Where grandpa
was so depressed at losing his
horses that for five years all he could do was
dream about opening a kaolin mine and collect
stamps, then finally had to give up
even his flat? Dear heart,
we have four children in the house, the tablecloth
whispered. I went pale. I never
imagined anything this
horrible could ever really
happen to me. So, once among the Slavs

143

I immediately gambled away Perspektive.
To avoid having to stare at those torturous
repeating episodes, when you first rent
a room to Madame Scriabine, then another to
someone who constantly
bangs the door shut. Not to mention the third and
fourth. The fifth one uses your cellar to chop up your
wife, instead of firewood. And it's clear
you have absolutely no other
choice but to sell
your stamps, hire a
cab, keep an eye on the
packing and single-handedly scrawl
Mitgepäck on the wood. Even now I can scarcely
believe I could be such an idiot, trying
for years to enlighten a
country where since time
immemorial everything was clear
in advance, especially the fact that you
deserved me! But let's put aside
History. I disappointed
Zwitter with it long ago. This poem has a purely
practical purpose, which is:
to persuade my current wife, Metka
Krašovec, not to forbid me
the young thoroughbred creatures I
race and bet on.
Last night in three hours I lost 219
dollars and won 240.
Whatever I do! My balance comes out on the
plus side!
21 dollars!
21 years!
It all evens out.
Whom did Lord Byron love?

my bard and brother

As the
chauffeur silkenly drives me
down to the city at four thirty, I
worry that downtown will slit my
throat. Thomas Smith, father of
Tony, alias Antonio Smith, best friend of
Goran and Boris, the twins and brothers
of Sofija, who
nearly became my
wife in Mexico.
Does my car
really have darkened windows? I'm
off to a bar where the drinks
are cheap between four and six. What they call
happy hours. Miss Miller is at
Bled now, at the dacha. That's also the name of
my beer. Metka, is she a
drag? And I drink:
beer after beer, quarter after
quarter lost to the
juke box. Joe and Mary are both so
beautiful I'm afraid they'll break my
shirt. And I think of
Braco. I don't even have his address.
People! Why do you
grow up!
Then I think, when I get to
Ljubljana, I'll put out an
ad. I've come back, Tomaž
Šalamun, making books and children is my
trade. I also want

four, like my
father. Call
three two four two zero three.
Joe has a different dog today and
great luck at darts.
Then a very strange, decidedly
hysterical laughter pierces the noise and refrigerated
air, like Fontana. Mary calls out:
LAST CALL HAPPY HOURS!
And I leap into
the sun and then over
Broadway back into the
air-conditioned limo, which takes me back to the castle.

chez les contents

Hey, old Triestine love, whom I
exported first to Brussels, then
California, then Jersualem: they say
you have a house on Mali Lošinj. Why didn't you
send me chocolates in Sarajevo?
Slim told me. He knows everything, even
all the dirt about my present
life. Come to Male Srakane
sometime with the boat. On the island I silently
glide from sheep to sheep, and shine a flashlight in
their mouths. And type in the shade under the reeds.
Beside me sits a creature that's lost its mind.
He wears a baseball cap and is covered in a
sheet. Slime oozes from his ears and eyes.
The people here constantly inter-
marry and abandon their offspring on the way.
So why didn't you send me chocolates in
Sarajevo? I'd like to see how your
son has grown up and if you still
agree with the original design for Poker.

small wonder that our old professor is now mayor of rome

I sat on a wall and sketched Perugia.
Argan also drops some coins in the almsbox.
For lunch at the pensione they give us cat meat,
at least that's what they say. I get better.
I'll never pass that exam.
Braco is in love with Vera, am I in love with Tatyana
or with Vera? Or with Dunya?
But not the Dunya who was in Perugia
and is an opera singer now, rather the Dunya
I was with at camp.
Vera and I saw each other in Greece.
Braco and I never saw each other at
camp. The English woman says
driving lessons here are practically free.
Tone will be the cause of our breaking up. Don't even
know how to use an eraser. In
Split Dikan stole Vera from me.
My surveyor abandons me in Orvieto.
I watch the people burning in hell.
They're naked and touching each other and then
they are included in frescoes and then Western
civilization clearly has nothing to point to
but a brothel
and in churches at that.

dear metka!

There are fresh flowers on my table every morning.
Now they change them in their big vases
every other day. For breakfast I sit at the
Quiet Table, so I just raise a hand and
wiggle my fingers to greet people
because I'm afraid of losing my metaphysics
if I say good morning. No one here
suffers because of you or Alejandro.
I'm always telling Trisha, Allan and
Kathy I'm afraid you won't get very
much out of me, I'm just married —
April 11 — and on the way to be with my
Mexican lover. Everyone here likes you.
I dance with Kathy, walk with Allan through the
fireflies — we stroll through woods like a
carpet — and admire Trisha enormously
for her paintings. When I make love to her,
I become a tree she's painting. Don't be
sad if I repeat that I won't
be able to live with you "faithfully,"
as people put it. I've tried, and
changed my plans. I'll be in Mexico
from the twenty-second to the twenty-ninth,
not from the twenty-ninth to the sixth.
That way the week before I fly to
Ljubljana I'll be back here to rest and it won't
be like when I flew back for the
wedding, when between the moment I

knocked on the door on
Dalmatin Street and the moment I
good-naturedly shoved Alejandro out of bed on
Salina Cruz only fourteen hours elapsed.
I'm afraid it would
scare you to death, same as then.

liberty, blue folder

My life is in a cage.
Others look after me.
Kansas has the same sort of dust as Pannonia.
All the stalks have burnt out in my throat.
I'd like to be modest and tiny and
compressed. I'd like to be
dead.
I read a precise list of the tips and
clothes my travel agent from Liberty
requires.
I can't afford them.
What is San Miguel de Allende like?
I carry the flag at such high speed that you
can't even hear when it pops.
Kings fall, shot down by mufflers.
At the airport I always eat the last
sandwich. I stare at its geological
strata. My skin smells like an egg,
golden. Why doesn't that fountain in the castle stop? White marble
putto, don't ever wake up!
In Ljubljana I lived in Gradišče.
Even there two children chained my windows with
clay hairs.
Will I ever walk past there?
Will I ever look in on my bay window?
Last time I almost ran down
Marko in a white crosswalk. Why did I burn
the prayers I'd written in
Iowa when Tone was killed? So as not to
hurt Nina?

I'm writing this poem in a hotel in Río
Lerma while Alejandro sleeps.
Nina nana,
for the children of the monogram a stranger.

la lettre de mon père, le pédiatre

June 14. Dear Tomaž,
Thank you for the congratulations. As for the
whirlpool of poetry pulling you
in — as for the group
of your altitude, privileged and
protected — I firmly hope it won't
explode you. The forces I would have
to muster —
after the explosion —
would be too little
for Metka and consequently also for you.
Today rain soaked the cedar at
Markovec — a drought till now had
damaged it —
and we hadn't watered it enough.
All best wishes
for you and Metka Yours Dad.
Nota: tu vois!
Sans changer un mot,
Doctor-in-Chief!
J'adore ton appétit!
Alas, I have no time
now to wonder about
your mysterious
mountain excursions and teas
with my wife.
I'm too entangled in my own
carnal business.
Let me congratulate you again.
This time for your
Ribičič Awards.

grain

In America Rose Kennedy goes to mass twice
each morning. Along the way she eats a sandwich
to save money. Three sons, three hero's medals
jingle on her blue blouse.
The woman even eats through the exaltation of the host.
All other women who don't eat through the
exaltation drown at
Chappaquidick, or go to hospitals for
electroshock. The third generation of Kennedys
numbers roughly a billion. They're sweeter than the
kitchiest picture postcards. Teddy
sails. He hasn't yet made up his mind. If America
fails, it will be because Teddy gets
mad at some prankster who breaks his sail's
frame. Meanwhile, in California my friend
Jerry Brown is sleeping sweetly. No
wonder he's rested. I make love to him night and day.
And somewhere, in America's heart, lost
amid the corn, an ordinary farmer says:
I've had it with this Boston quasi-elite
and their provincial Catholic bullshit.
To hell with Teddy and his health care
mafia! In green fields and in the
blue sky my most secret flower
opens. That's also how every young
Slovenian poet should behave,
and if not, then in this century they simply
do not have a chance.

the word and the truth

Whoever heeds the suffering of women is no
genius. Back to Mexico, back to Meeejico!
Who guides my fate, my stallion!
Precise are the time and the place where he

wounds me. Kneel stallion, so I can
kneel, too. Rise up, Other! Mine is just
the technique. Arranging the groomsmen to
carry my saddle from murdered trails.

It's true. In the end, when the harmonica
plays, the medallion's beauty will decide.
But the condition is awful. Music! At your

fall I didn't hear it. Let the farewell be
for you, then, Blind to Color. Whoever ignores
the movement of shadows is wiped out for my freedom.

September 11, 1979

Tomaž Šalamun was born in 1941 in Zagreb, Croatia and raised in Koper, Slovenia. He has a degree in Art History from the University of Ljubljana, and before devoting himself to poetry he worked as a conceptual artist. Since the publication in 1966 of his first book, *Poker*, he has published thirty collections of poetry in his home country and is now recognized as one of the leading poets in Europe. His honors include the Prešeren Fund Prize, the Jenko Prize, a Pushcart Prize, a visiting Fulbright to Columbia University, and a fellowship to the International Writing Program at the University of Iowa. He has also served as Cultural Attaché to the Slovenian Consulate in New York. Besides having his work appear in numerous journals internationally, he has had four collections of selected poetry published in English: *The Selected Poems of Tomaž Šalamun* (The Ecco Press, 1988); *The Shepherd, The Hunter* (Pedernal Press, 1992); *The Four Questions of Melancholy* (White Pine Press, 1997); and *Feast* (Harcourt Brace, 2000). He is married to the painter Metka Krašovec.

Michael Biggins is Slavic and East European studies librarian at the University of Washington Libraries in Seattle. His translations include the novels *Northern Lights* and *Mocking Desire* by Drago Jančar, a memoir by Boris Pahor titled *Pilgrim Among the Shadows*, and a number of shorter pieces from Slovenian and Russian.

A BALLAD FOR METKA KRAŠOVEC was originally published in Slovenian
as *Balada za Metko Krašovec* (Ljubljana: Državna založba Slovenije, 1981)
Photos on front and back cover appear courtesy of the author
Text set in Janson, headings in Arial Narrow
Designed by Chaim
This is a first English edition published in 2001 by
Twisted Spoon Press
P.O. Box 21 – Preslova 12, 150 21 Prague 5, Czech Republic
info@twistedspoon.com / www.twistedspoon.com
Printed and bound in the Czech Republic by Tiskárny Havlíčkův Brod

ACKNOWLEDGMENTS: Some poems have appeared previously in *The Four
Questions of Melancholy* (Fredonia: White Pine Press, 1997) and in the
following journals: *Denver Quarterly*, *Poetry Miscellany*, and *Willow Springs*.
"When I crawl ..." appears in *Feast*, edited by Charles Simic (New York:
Harcourt Brace, 2000).
The author wishes to express his heartfelt gratitude to YADDO.
The publisher would like to thank Jeffrey Young and Aleš Šteger for making
this project possible, and Ken Ganfield, Jon Mooallem, and Pavel Rut for
their help.

Distributed in North America by SCB Distributors
15608 South New Century Drive, Gardena, CA 90248, USA
toll free: 1-800-729-6423 / info@scbdistributors.com